A
Bright
Idea

By Susan Ring

CELEBRATION PRESS
Pearson Learning Group

The following people from **Pearson Learning Group**
have contributed to the development of this product:

Joan Mazzeo, Dorothea Fox **Design** | **Editorial** Leslie Feierstone-Barna, Cindy Kane
Christine Fleming **Marketing** | **Publishing Operations** Jennifer Van Der Heide
Production Laura Benford-Sullivan
Content Area Consultant Dr. Amy Rabb-Liu and Dr. Charles Liu

The following people from **DK** have
contributed to the development of this product:

Art Director Rachael Foster

Martin Wilson **Managing Art Editor** | **Managing Editor** Marie Greenwood
Spencer Holbrook **Design** | **Editorial** Julie Ferris
Brenda Clynch **Picture Research** | **Production** Gordana Simakovic
Richard Czapnik, Andy Smith **Cover Design** | **DTP** David McDonald
Consultant David Glover

Dorling Kindersley would like to thank: Peter Bull for original artwork and Ed Merritt for cartography. Rose Horridge, Gemma Woodward, and Hayley Smith in the DK Picture Library. Johnny Pau for additional cover design work.

Picture Credits: AKG: 15t, 17. The Art Archive: Ara Collection Paris/Dagli Orti 8t. Bridgeman Art Library: Guildhall Library, Corporation of London, UK 8b. Corbis: 23t; Bettmann 14b; Philip James Corwin 31t; Macduff Everton 10r; Walter Hodges 28; Hulton Collection 20b, 31cc; Lester Lefkowitz 30t; Charles Michael Murray 6r; Francesca Muntada 29t; James Noble 1; Owaki – Kulla 26t; Schenectady Museum, Hall of Electrical History Foundation 16t, 16b; Francisco Villaflor 30tcl; Adam Woolfitt 19l. Courtesy conEdison 24b. Courtesy The Canadian Intellectual Property Office 14t, 30bl. Courtesy The Patent Office, UK 13b. Edisonian LLC: 18r. Getty Images: Stone/Ken Biggs 3. John Frost Newspaper Collection 26b. Kamstrup Precision 22bl. Mary Evans Picture Library: 11tr, 12r, 13t, 22br, 30ccl, 30ccr. Masterfile: J.A. Kraulis 4–5. Rex Features: SKC 7c. The Science Museum, London: 10l, 11l, 12l, 15bl, 19r, 22t, 27tl, 27cl, 30ccc, 30bc, 30br, 31tcr. Science & Society Picture Library 25b, 27bl. Science Photo Library: Hank Morgan 29b. The Smithsonian Institute: 20t, 21b, 24t. Union Pacific Historical Collection 21t, 31bl. U.S. Department of the Interior, National Park Service: Edison National Historic Site 18l. Jacket: Corbis/Walter Hodges t.

All other images: 🕮 Dorling Kindersley © 2005. For further information see www.dkimages.com

ISBN: 0-7652-5266-X

Color reproduction by Colourscan, Singapore
Printed in the United States of America
2 3 4 5 6 7 8 9 10   08 07 06 05

1-800-321-3106
www.pearsonlearning.com

Contents

Life Before the Light Bulb

Suppose that it's the middle of the night and you are staying at a relative's house. You need to get a glass of water, but the house is dark and unfamiliar. What would you do? Most likely you would turn on a light to find the kitchen or bathroom. After getting yourself a drink, you would switch off the lights as you returned to bed.

Now suppose what life would be like if you could not easily turn lights on and off as you needed them. You might have to rely on the Sun and the Moon as your main sources of light. That's what it was like for people thousands of years ago. Light bulbs and electricity did not exist. Although early people had probably discovered fire, they had to learn how to control it to provide light when and where it was needed.

Over thousands of years, people developed different light sources that led to the electric lights we have today. This is the story of those developments and how they changed human life and civilization.

Fire was the first light source people were able to control. Scientists believe that this happened around 100,000 years ago. Most likely, a person first lit a branch or stick from a natural source, such as a smoldering tree that had been struck by lightning, and then learned to maintain the flame. Fire then provided people with a consistent light source. It also gave them warmth. Because animals were often afraid of fire, it kept early humans safer as well.

The ability to control fire was probably the first step toward human civilization. By spending time together around the fire, people built a sense of community. Extended hours of light may also have helped people to make better tools, plan for hunts, and cook foods.

A campfire kept early people warm, provided safety from wild animals, and lengthened working hours by providing light.

First Light Sources

The first fires were probably located in one spot or hearth, around which people gathered. However, evidence shows that early people soon discovered how to carry fire with them. They made torches from sticks or reeds dipped in animal fat. Although these torches provided a handy light source, the open flames could be dangerous. In addition, a torch large enough to provide light for any length of time was probably heavy and hard to handle.

Stones were hollowed out to make crude lamps.

Then, about 70,000 years ago, people began to make the first lamps. They used hard stone pounding tools to form hollow areas in softer stones, collected shells, or shaped and dried clay. Then they poured animal fat into the hollow and added moss or straw. The moss or straw absorbed the fat and held the flame. This is similar to how a wick, the string in a candle or an oil lamp, absorbs the wax or oil that keeps a flame burning.

A shell could be used as a lamp by adding oil and a wick.

Pottery oil lamps were used in ancient Rome.

Candles

Between 3000 B.C. and 2000 B.C., people in Egypt made torches called rushlights by soaking the core of reeds in animal fat. Although rushlights were the predecessors of candles, they did not have true wicks, which allow candles to burn longer. The Romans were the first to weave fibers together and use them as candle wicks. In fact, the word *candle* comes from *candere*, a Latin word meaning "to shine."

Ancient candles and lamps primarily used tallow—animal fat—for fuel, but tallow gave off a strong smell when it burned. By the fourth century A.D., people in China began making candles from beeswax, the substance secreted by honeybees to make honeycombs. Beeswax was a much better fuel than tallow because it smelled better and was not as smoky. Beeswax candles were very expensive, though, so only wealthy people could afford them. In the late eighteenth century, candles made from spermaceti, or whale oil, were introduced. These candles were not as expensive as beeswax candles, so more people could afford to use them.

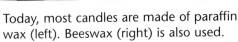

Today, most candles are made of paraffin wax (left). Beeswax (right) is also used.

The Search for a Better Light

early gas lamp

During the late eighteenth and early nineteenth centuries, some new and cheaper sources of lighting were developed. Fossil fuels, such as petroleum and coal, found deep in the earth, became especially popular.

In 1792, Scottish engineer William Murdock began experimenting with coal gas, which was produced by heating coal. At first, he used the gas to light lanterns around his home and his company's factory. By 1804, Murdock had placed 900 gaslights in cotton mills and had become known as the father of the gas industry.

In 1821, natural gas began to gain popularity. It worked much like coal gas, but natural gas forms inside the earth and does not need to be manufactured. One of the first places to use natural gas was Fredonia, New York. Natural gas from a 27-foot-deep well was piped to buildings and used for light. Some places, however, did not have natural gas deposits and so could not take advantage of this fuel.

Gas lighting changed the look of London, England, and many other cities.

Early Experiments in Electricity

Electricity is found in many forms. It appears in the sky as powerful lightning bolts. It darts through the human body as nerve impulses. Electric pulses are also used by animals such as the electric ray to stun prey.

As far back as the fifth and sixth centuries B.C., people tried to understand the nature of electricity. In 600 B.C., Thales, a Greek mathematician, became curious about what is now known as static electricity. Thales rubbed wool over a piece of amber (a yellowish substance usually made of fossilized tree resin or sap). He discovered that once amber had been rubbed, it acquired static electricity and could attract lightweight objects such as straw, feathers, and hair.

When rubbed, amber acquires static electricity and can attract lightweight objects. The Greek word for *amber* is *elektron*, which is the origin of the word *electricity*.

Electric rays use electric pulses to stun their prey.

Electricity: Static vs. Current

Static electricity consists of charges that do not flow. When a person or thing comes into contact with an object holding static electricity, there is a discharge, causing a shock. On the other hand, current electricity flows through wires. It can be generated in a battery or by a generator powered by steam, oil, or other fuels. It can then be sent to power such items as radios, televisions, and computers.

Collecting Electrical Charges

The Leyden jar, first used in the Netherlands in 1746, was developed by early experimenters to store electric charges.

In the mid-1700s, Dutch scientists worked on ways to collect and store energy. They invented the Leyden jar, which was a glass container with metal foil on the inside and outside. The top of the jar was placed against a machine that generated static electricity, which was then collected in the jar. The static electricity remained in the jar until a wire (or anything that conducts electricity) touched the inside and outside foil—which caused the electricity to discharge, creating sparks.

In 1747, American scientist and inventor Benjamin Franklin experimented with electricity. Franklin noticed the similarities between the Leyden jar's tiny sparks and the giant sparks made by lightning. He thought they might both be forms of electricity, even though they were different in power and size.

Franklin's experiments with electricity also led to his invention of the lightning rod in 1752. This metal rod attracts static electricity from a storm cloud. Because it draws lightning and is placed higher than other buildings around it, it protects buildings and people from being struck by lightning.

A lightning rod draws the charge from a storm cloud and conducts it into the ground, thus protecting buildings from taking the charge and possibly catching fire.

The First Battery

Italian scientist Count Alessandro Volta was also curious about the mysterious properties of electricity. He wanted to store an electric charge, but he also wanted to produce a steady flow of electricity. The Leyden jar could only give off short bursts of electric sparks.

Count Alessandro Volta

In 1800, Volta invented the Voltaic Pile. This device, made of copper and zinc disks, had pasteboard soaked in salt water in between the disks. Volta stacked the disks about 12 inches high. At the bottom of the stack was a copper disk—the positive terminal of the pile. At the top was a zinc disk—the negative terminal. The stack was held together by three glass rods. Volta showed that a low current of electricity flowed from the device when a wire was attached to either end. He had made the first chemical battery and, for the first time, showed how to produce a continuous electric current.

Voltaic Pile

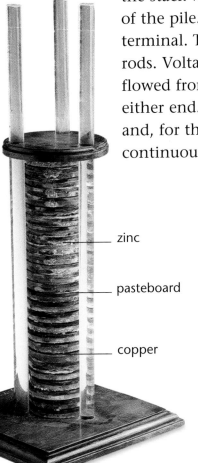

zinc

pasteboard

copper

How a Battery Works

Volta showed that stacking two different metals, each separated only by a moist, porous material, causes a chemical reaction that generates electricity. Today, batteries are made with many combinations of elements. Like Volta's pile, however, they all have negative and positive terminals. The unit of electric potential is the volt, named after the Count.

An Arc of Light

Humphry Davy, an English chemist, invented the first electric light. In 1809, he connected one wire to the negative terminal of a huge Voltaic Pile and another wire to the positive terminal. Then, between the other ends of the wires he placed a charcoal strip. (Charcoal is made mostly of carbon and is created by burning wood or other material.) The charcoal glowed, demonstrating that battery (electric) power could be used to produce light. He also passed an electric current through many other materials. When he passed it through a platinum wire, the wire glowed.

Through his many experiments, Davy discovered that if he ran an electric current through two charcoal rods placed slightly apart, a curved band of electric current jumped from one rod to the other. This discovery, called an electric arc, eventually led to arc lamps, which were first used in a lighthouse in 1862. They gave off a very bright, white light.

This arc lamp dates from the 1870s.

Humphry Davy gave public lectures to demonstrate how the arc lamp worked.

The Light Bulb Is Born

Warren de la Rue

In 1820, British scientist Warren de la Rue placed a platinum coil in an airless glass tube. He knew that platinum had a very high melting point and believed that it would not melt when an electric current was passed through it. He also thought that if he removed the air from the tube, or created a vacuum, the platinum would not catch fire. Air, after all, is needed for burning. The scientist had made the first incandescent light bulb, which means its light was made by heating a material until it glowed. Unfortunately, platinum was too expensive for de la Rue's light bulb to be of any practical use.

About 20 years later, an Englishman named Frederick de Moleyns also created a light bulb, which he patented. His light bulb also used an airless glass tube, but de Moleyns placed powdered charcoal between two platinum wires. One problem with de Moleyns' bulb was that the charcoal completely blackened the glass as it burned, quickly dimming the light.

What Are Patents?

A patent is a legal protection granted by the government to safeguard a citizen's ideas and inventions. If someone copies a patented invention without permission, the inventor may sue or take other legal action. Patents allow people to share their ideas and inventions with society free from the fear that others might steal them and unjustly make money from them.

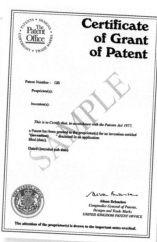

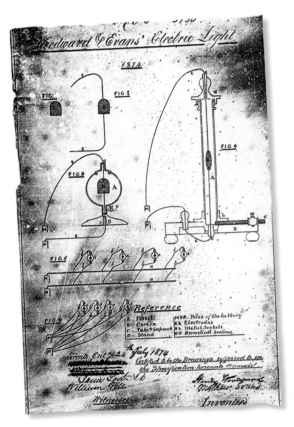

Woodward's and Evans' patent included detailed drawings of their invention.

In 1874, Henry Woodward and Matthew Evans of Canada filed a Canadian patent for their version of the incandescent bulb. In 1876, they obtained a U.S. patent on what they now called the electric lamp. To create light, the Canadian team used a threadlike piece of carbon that would glow when an electric current was passed through it. Their glass bulb was filled with nitrogen gas to prevent the carbon strip from burning up.

Unfortunately, Woodward and Evans did not have enough money to perfect their invention. In 1879, American inventor Thomas Edison, who had developed similar ideas, purchased the U.S. patent from the inventors. With the support of wealthy investors, such as the Vanderbilts and J. P. Morgan, Edison began the Edison Electric Light Company to further develop his ideas.

Thomas Edison purchased the Canadians' patent and founded the Edison Electric Light Company. This product label shows Edison with his inventions.

The Modern Light Bulb

Joseph Swan demonstrated his light bulb in England in 1878.

Although Thomas Edison is often credited with inventing the light bulb, British scientist Joseph Swan also patented a version of the incandescent light bulb. He received his patent in 1878—ten months before Edison received his. Swan had begun work on his bulb in 1860. It featured an almost airless tube and a carbon fiber filament. Though his bulb worked, it had a short lifespan, and the light it produced was very dim. These weaknesses were caused by several problems. First, the vacuum pumps Swan used did not remove enough air from the bulb. The presence of oxygen caused the filament to burn up quickly. Second, the material the filament was made from required a great deal of electric current to run through it before it became hot and glowed. Finally, Swan's power source was a battery, which was not strong enough to produce a bright light.

What Is a Filament?

The material that glows in the center of a light bulb is called a filament. Early light bulbs had carbon filaments. Today, filaments are made from the metal tungsten, which was discovered in 1783. Edison considered using tungsten as a filament in the 1880s, but the brittle metal was hard to work with.

Swan's bulb had a carbon filament.

Most modern bulbs have tungsten filaments.

Edison Improves the Light Bulb

Edison's Menlo Park research team

In the same year that Joseph Swan patented his light bulb, Edison told a *New York Sun* newspaper reporter that he was sure that he could create a light that everybody would use. Even though several kinds of incandescent bulbs had been invented, most homes and streets were still lit by gas because none of the bulbs worked very well. All the previous work on light bulbs, however, gave Edison clues about the approaches his research team should and should not take.

Edison's Invention Factory

Edison's laboratory was stocked with many books, tools, and chemicals. About an hour away from the hustle and bustle of New York City, Menlo Park provided a perfect environment for creative thinking.

The Menlo Park Team

Edison assembled a team of experts to assist him in his laboratory in Menlo Park, New Jersey. From 1878 to 1880, the scientists worked tirelessly to perfect an incandescent light bulb. The hardest part of their job was determining which material worked best as a filament. Edison knew that anything with carbon would eventually burn up, but he wanted to find the substance that would glow the longest.

The Menlo Park team tried thousands of fibers—everything from human hair to fishing line to spider webs. Edison even had samples of vegetable and plant fibers sent to him from around the world. Each fiber had to be made as thin as thread and baked until it was black with carbon. Edison experimented with thousands of materials—more than 6,000 plants alone—to determine which would let the bulb glow for an extended period of time.

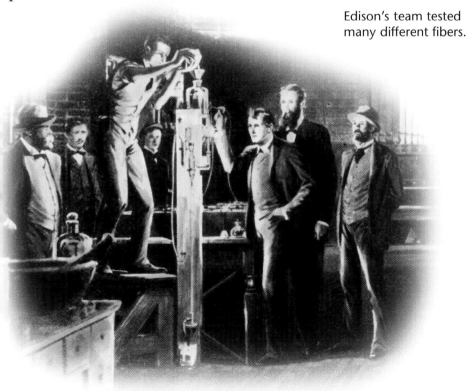

Edison's team tested many different fibers.

On the Right Track

Edison kept the team working day and night on delicate, painstaking experiments. Finally, in October 1879, they tried a carbonized cotton thread filament that glowed for nearly 15 hours. Edison knew that he was at last on the right track. No other material had glowed nearly as long.

By the end of 1880, Edison and his Menlo Park team had produced a bulb that burned for more than 200 hours! They used Japanese bamboo in a strong vacuum to produce such a long-lasting bulb. The team was well on its way to developing the modern light bulb.

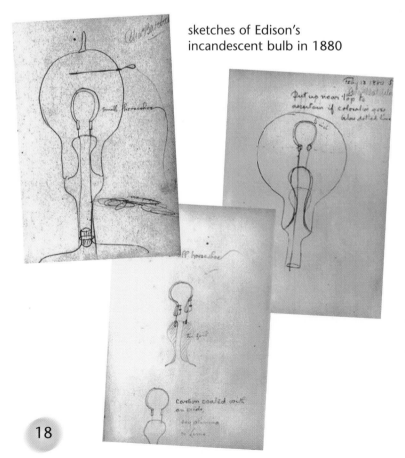

sketches of Edison's incandescent bulb in 1880

Perfecting the Pump

Finding a good filament was not the team's only challenge. Many glass bulbs were needed for experiments, so Edison had to hire glassblowers. A filament then had to be carefully inserted into each bulb before the air could be removed and the base sealed.

Although Swan had developed a good vacuum pump in 1878, the pump still left a small amount of air in the bulbs. Edison realized that any air would speed up destruction of the filament. As a result, his research team made important improvements to Swan's pump. Eventually they were able to create a very strong vacuum in each bulb.

This version of Edison's lamp was made in 1880.

Glassblowing

In the late 1800s, glass was still being made by hand. The glassblower blew air into a hollow metal rod with a glob of red-hot liquid glass on its end. The glass was then carefully shaped with special tools and cooled until it was hard. Today, glassblowing survives mostly as an art form.

Spreading the Word

Edison was very famous and was frequently featured in the press.

Thomas Edison knew that in order to sell his light bulbs he had to let people everywhere know about his invention. When J. P. Morgan and the Vanderbilts first invested in this invention, they expected Edison to develop a product that would make money.

Most people of the time were not familiar with electric lighting, except for arc lamps. The dangers of electricity and wires, moreover, were a little frightening to the public. Still, Edison hoped to make his newly improved light bulb something that people would want to use in their homes and businesses. On December 21, 1879, he ran the first public notice about the incandescent light bulb in the *New York Herald*.

Edison also wanted people to see firsthand what his light bulb could do. On New Year's Eve in 1879, more than 3,000 people came to Menlo Park to see the laboratory illuminated with twenty-five warmly glowing incandescent light bulbs. This event was the first of many to present electric lighting to the public.

Before electric lights, every evening at dusk, street lighters had to light the gas lamps that lined city streets.

The SS *Columbia* was the first commercial user of Edison's light bulb. At night it was brightly illuminated by 150 lights.

In 1880, Edison had another opportunity to advertise the light bulb. One of his financial supporters, Henry Villard, asked him to furnish the new steamship SS *Columbia* with electric lighting. As the ship sailed around South America, people at each port came to see the magically lit boat.

However, Edison faced a setback that same year when Joseph Swan sued him for using his light bulb design, which was patented. The British courts ruled in Swan's favor. They believed that Swan should receive money and recognition for his design from Edison. Edison was required to make Swan a partner in his British electric works. The company was renamed the Edison and Swan United Electric Company.

Although Swan was the one to receive the patent for the light bulb, Edison improved it dramatically. He created a light bulb that was easy to use and affordable for the average person. His achievement changed the world.

This sketch was prepared for a sign showing Edison's name in lights. The inventor produced the sign and displayed it at the Crystal Palace in London.

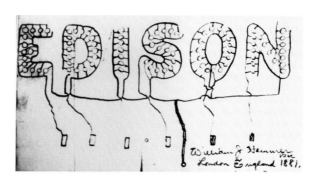

vering the Light Bulb

The dramatic lighting of the SS *Columbia* was a huge success. It helped to spark the public's interest in incandescent lighting.

It also allowed Edison to turn his attention to designing electric power sources and ways to deliver power to customers. The electricity for the SS *Columbia* was generated by a single plant on the bottom floor of the ship. Edison's main interest, however, was to develop central plants, which could deliver electricity to widely scattered areas.

early electric meter

The inventor began to map out a plan for delivering electricity to the general population. First,

electric meter today

Edison created a meter, based on the design of existing gas meters, to measure electricity usage. People could then be billed for the exact amount of power they used. Second, Edison's team used a network of wires to carry the electricity from a central plant to its customers.

reading an electric meter in the 1880s

The Edison team worked around the clock, often sleeping only three or four hours each night. They had to create powerful generators to make the electricity. Lighting fixtures, safety switches, and fuse boxes were invented along with other items. Edison also continued to improve the light bulb itself, looking for longer-lasting and cheaper materials.

As the initial planning drew to a close, Edison decided that a section of Lower Manhattan in New York City called the First District would be a good place to install his first large electric plant. Edison chose New York City because many of his investors were there, and he thought the city would be a good location to show how a delivery system connected to a central plant worked.

the generator for Edison's first electric plant

Pearl Street Station began with one generator, which produced power for 800 electric light bulbs. Within 14 months, over 12,000 bulbs were aglow. However, with Edison's direct current system, the voltage dropped as distance from the generator increased. Plants had to be built close to users. This was costly and soon led to the development of better systems by rival companies.

Pearl Street Power Station

The power station was a huge undertaking. First, a location was chosen for the huge steam generators that would make the electricity. The team decided on Pearl Street in Lower Manhattan. Then wires were laced along telegraph poles, and holes were dug in the city streets for underground cables to deliver the electricity. Finally, the First District's buildings themselves were wired.

On September 4, 1882, Edison flipped a switch in J. P. Morgan's office. For the first time, electric power flowed to the homes and businesses of the First District, setting the neighborhood aglow with incandescent light.

By the end of the 1880s, electric lights were being used 24 hours a day, particularly for transportation and business needs. Edison had proved that his power and electric lighting system could work on a large scale. The inventor told a newspaper reporter, "I have accomplished all I promised." In the United States, the name Edison Electric Light Company would later be changed to General Electric.

model of the Pearl Street Power Station in New York City

Roads in the First District were dug up so that underground cables could be laid down.

Generating Power

A generator converts the energy of motion into electricity through a process called electromagnetic induction. The process involves the following steps.

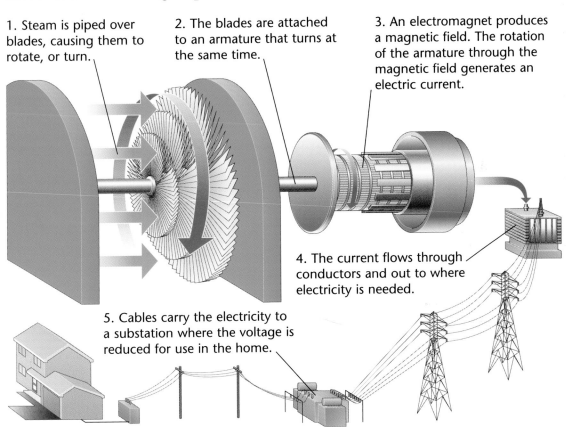

1. Steam is piped over blades, causing them to rotate, or turn.

2. The blades are attached to an armature that turns at the same time.

3. An electromagnet produces a magnetic field. The rotation of the armature through the magnetic field generates an electric current.

4. The current flows through conductors and out to where electricity is needed.

5. Cables carry the electricity to a substation where the voltage is reduced for use in the home.

Portable Generators

Some early generators were small enough to be pulled by horses to the location where a power source was needed. This generator, made by Charles Parsons, was used in England to light up a pond for night skating.

Electricity Changes the World

From 1879 to 1882, the number of customers that used Thomas Edison's light bulbs totaled 203. That number increased to 710 by 1889 and by 1899 had soared to three million customers.

Incandescent lights set streets, hospitals, schools, and offices aglow. People began to make huge changes in the way they lived. After dark they could finally continue activities that needed light, such as reading and sewing, without eyestrain or worry about the dangers of gas explosions.

Electricity was soon used for more than just lighting. Electric water pumps and elevators were invented. These innovations made the first skyscrapers possible. In less than twenty years, the electric light and the new electric power industry had totally changed the world.

Electricity enabled builders to construct huge skyscrapers.

Edison's Death

Thomas Edison died on October 18, 1931, at the age of eighty-four. President Herbert Hoover asked U.S. citizens to dim their lights at ten o'clock that evening in honor of the great inventor.

THE DAILY MIRROR   Monday, October 19, 1931

EDISON, THE WORLD'S GREATEST INVENTOR, DEAD

GENIUS WHOSE DISCOVERIES
TRANSFORMED OUR LIVES

Made Electricity, Moving Pictures and Telephones Realities to All

Thomas Alva Edison, the greatest inventor the world has ever known, died early yesterday at his home in West Orange, New Jersey, U.S.A., aged eighty-four. ... had been in a state of ... three days ... away in his sleep. Mrs. ...

Electricity in the Home

the early twentieth century, many different kinds of electric gadgets, such as those shown below, were invented.

tea maker

electric heater

food mixer

One major factor slowed the placing of electric lights in homes: the cost of installing wiring. However, people became more willing to invest in wiring when they realized it would allow for many conveniences in addition to lighting. At the end of the nineteenth and beginning of the twentieth centuries, all kinds of electric appliances were being invented.

Many electric inventions made housework easier and life more pleasant. Personal grooming appliances started to appear. Electric heaters and fans were introduced to control temperature. Today, new or improved electric appliances for the home are invented every year.

Today, we rely on electricity for equipment such as computers.

Electric Invention	Year Invented
Iron	1882
Fan	1886
Hairdryer	1890
Stove	1891
Toaster	1893
Washing machine	1908
Electric heating	1916

Lighting Today

Since the days of Edison, light fixtures and bulbs have continued to evolve. In 1910, the American inventor William Coolidge improved on the General Electric Company's method of making tungsten light bulb filaments. Because of its high melting point, tungsten has turned out to be the best filament material yet discovered. With Coolidge's improvements, tungsten became more affordable. Today, most light bulbs have tungsten filaments.

Fluorescent and neon light bulbs are also available. Instead of using a filament within a vacuum, an electric current is passed through a low-pressure gas. The energy of the current is converted to light by gas atoms. Flourescent and neon bulbs provide as much light as incandescent bulbs, yet they use less electricity. French scientist Alexandre Edmond Becquerel first created fluorescent bulbs in 1867. They were not introduced to the public, however, until the New York World's Fair of 1938–1939.

Halogen lamps are incandescent lights that have a tungsten filament. The presence of halogen in the bulb allows the filament to run at a higher temperature than in a conventional bulb, so the light is brighter.

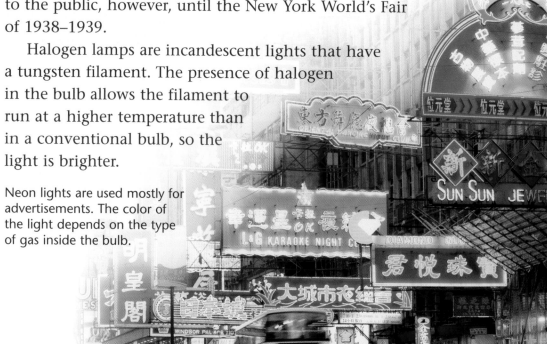

Neon lights are used mostly for advertisements. The color of the light depends on the type of gas inside the bulb.

ergy and the Environment

Today, lighting and appliances create huge demands for electric power. Think about how many inventions, including cars, refrigerators, and ovens, use light bulbs.

As a result, great amounts of fossil fuels are burned to generate electricity. Fossil fuels are nonrenewable energy sources because once they are burned, they are hard to replace. Moreover, carbon dioxide gas is released into the air, which contributes to global warming.

Wind, water, and solar power are renewable energy sources because they do not get used up in the same way as fossil fuels, such as oil and coal, do. All over the world, people are trying to develop ways to use these power sources instead of fossil fuels. Hydroelectric dams, for example, use moving water to generate power.

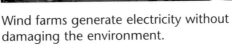
Wind farms generate electricity without damaging the environment.

Solar panels are used to gather sunlight and turn the radiant energy into heat or electric energy. Solar power is a clean and practically limitless energy source. However, it is still costly to use in comparison to coal and oil.

The electricity that hydroelectric dams generate is no different than electricity made from fossil fuels. Yet these dams do not produce the emissions that come from burning fossil fuels. However, hydroelectric dams can present their own threats to the environment by affecting water flow rates and water temperatures.

Hydroelectric dams use water to generate electricity.

From Fire to the Light Bulb: A Timeline

3000 B.C. and earlier

The Sun, Moon, and fire are the main light sources until torches and stone lamps appear.

3000 B.C.–2000 B.C.

Wicks and candles are invented.

about 600 B.C.

The Greek mathematician Thales experiments with static electricity.

1800

Alessandro Volta of Italy creates the first battery, called the Voltaic Pile.

1809

Humphry Davy pioneers arc lighting in London, England.

1820

Warren de Rue makes first light b in London, England.

1874

Henry Woodward and Matthew Evans patent their light bulb in Canada.

1878

● Joseph Swan patents his incandescent light bulb.
● Edison Electric Light Company is founded in the United States.

1879

Thomas Edison introduces his incandescent light bulb.

Careful planning must be used no matter what kind of power source is developed. When the world finds more ways to use renewable energy sources, Earth will become a much cleaner and healthier planet.

No one knows exactly what light sources will be used in the future. One thing, however, is certain: People will always want more light in their lives, especially once the Sun has set.

1600s

Improvements are made in oil lamps and candles.

1700s

● William Murdock of Scotland uses coal gas to light his home and his company's factory.
● The Leyden jar is developed in the Netherlands.
● Benjamin Franklin experiments with electricity and invents the lightning rod in the United States.

1823

London streets are illuminated with gas lamps.

1841

Frederick de Moleyns of England receives the first light bulb patent.

1867

Alexandre Edmond Becquerel of France invents the fluorescent light bulb.

1880

Thomas Edison supplies an electric light system for the American ship SS Columbia.

1882

Thomas Edison opens the first electric power station in New York City.

1910

William Coolidge improves the tungsten filament, making its production more affordable.

31

Index